Interior Design for a New Life: the secrets and struggle of decorating for what is to come

by

Susan Devine Napoli

To: the do it yourself folks both the willing and the unwilling.

Special Dedication to: My fellow neighbors and friends in Houston, many of whom I have not met but have come together in solidarity to rebuild our great city after Hurricane Harvey. May this book inspire you and become a kind of wish book until you are able to rebuild. Sometimes in order to move to greater heights we have to take some steps backwards. Blessed be your process.

Passages from Psalm 139 of the bible are used in this book.

The photo on the cover is a stock photo and not one of my own place of residence.

Contents

***

Environments Matter

Environments matter, they just do. It matters where the seed drops that becomes a tree. There needs to be the right conditions. Water. Sun. Shade. Room to grow. It matters where animals live. They need food. Shelter. Freedom to roam. Others of their kind. I live near a nature preserve. After doing the history of the area, I have found that the area was never developed beyond the Native Americans and pioneering Settlers. Someone had foresight to save that tract of land. It is a place that children and adults learn about nature. To see native plants and animals in the environment they have always had. Surrounding that area are oil refineries to the north, a university to the south, and residential area that was built to house the manned space program known as NASA today. Any one of these could have taken over this land if it wasn't for the foresight of the individual, that soon became a committee with power. Because of that preserve, there are animals in the green spaces, inside the fence at NASA, an occasionally in the neighborhoods. It is not unusual to hear of a coyote sighting or an alligator as there is also a natural waterway to the bay that leads to the ocean. More commonly there are deer, opossum, and smaller animals. What is surprising to me is that not many either do not know of the nature preserve or how new the development of the area is. There was almost no development of the area until the gentleman who owned it struck oil. He was a rancher and had built his home on the banks of Clear Creek, a mansion by any standards, that still stands. After that, the land was sold for development which occurred in the 1960s. I mention that for one reason.

The animals themselves do not seem to mind sharing the space with people. The safety risk is low if you follow the rules to avoid how these animals would feel threatened. They love their environment. The people are not so sure.

Environments for people are a bit more complicated. People are very particular of their environments. It matters who people live with and work with. It matters what is said. It matters how resources are acquired and how they are distributed. It matters if they are allowed to grow and change. It is common that people find themselves in the wrong environment, venture out and find another that might be better suited. People find new jobs; they find new places to meet people. It happens all the time, if you take notice.

I am fascinated by environments, to look at them more closely and to build healthy ones. It has been a lifetime of noticing what goes into them and what makes me and others comfortable. I arranged my house and my classrooms using what I learned. It does matter how furniture is arranged for the activities you like to do. It matters in classrooms too...one of the most intriguing is that an unplanned environment can make children squabble over the toys and activities if it is not arranged carefully. I looked at that a long time. It was my favorite puzzle to solve. I found it was true. I then started building better environments for me. This is the story of my environments and the insight that went in my most recent one. The first one like it in 36 years. What a treat!

Part 1: Preparation

Not Interior Design

I came that close to studying interior design, three times. I even enrolled in a course and dropped it for reasons I was not sure. I have come to realize later that environments are about more than beauty and more than functionality. It is more than a place to eat, sleep, and rest. It is more than safety from the elements. It is a statement of who we are and reveals startling things to the visitors, sometimes. They interpret what they see and draw conclusions about us. There are even television shows about it. You can see it in the home improvement shows. The designer often asks as to why they have let things gotten the way they are and why they want to change it. They ask how they want it to look. Then the owner is whisked away and brought back to the reveal. They cry tears of joy and say this is how they wanted it. Or not. I have seen people go into shock too. That omg look that says how will I live with that element and nod and say they like it, it's different. Yeah, artistic license does not always know what the person really wants in their environment. Sometimes the person doesn't know either but it is not <u>that</u>. That element they don't like and are not sure why.

Thankfully for the field, if it can look like a magazine photo when they are done, the clients are over the moon about the results. They have something to brag about and for people in their lives to come see. It is clear that environments delight people.

For me, liking something or having it in my environment was sometimes temporary. I was in a process of self-discovery. As I found out more about myself, I would change the environment.

It was interior design of my own making by putting what I loved on display. I kept rearranging and even changing colors. I was someone they could not figure out. It was good really, I didn't know either. How could I tell them or anyone? I couldn't.

The Changing Environment

A changing environment to me is a good thing. It signals growth.

I have quite a lot of my early story in my book, <u>Tiny Living: from 1300 square feet to 400</u>, so I will go on from where that book ends. I am living in a minimal environment. I thought I was going to live in an RV and see the country. When I got a "no" on that plan, I moved into an 800 square foot apartment, massive for the amount of stuff I had. I wanted a quiet place to live and work. A place to figure things out. I could not move my furniture or a some of my stuff. I walked away with enough to get by on, the stuff I would have taken in an RV.

I am growing quite a bit in this environment. It has been deeply spiritual and insightful. It is changing as I change...what I want to have in my place and how I want to live. I am still purging, interestingly enough. I know it seems weird to keep purging stuff, but it is true. As one who is hooked on nostalgia and the items from my own past, I am not interested in those things so much anymore. I was encouraged to pack up my stuff and wait for a move in my quiet and prayer time. It is a time in my life I seek God for everything to get out of the mess I was in. Everything.

I loaded my car and got boxes. I lived with the most minimal of stuff. I threw out or donated what I did not really need or could fit into my car. It looked like I would leave in one car load. Then an interesting turn of events happened to help me realize that I was in this particular place for a reason. It was by design I was there. I did not like it at all, even though it was pointed out to me by a sign. Really big into signs, I got a literal one. It said. "free rent." Who can pass that up? I got 22 free days until I could pay. It was chaotic and loud. Then they sold it and began making changes. It got better by the day. I wanted to leave anyway. Then my eyes were opened to what I had. I became very appreciative. I realized I would have to stay, so I began to make it a home. Then I was hit with insight that I did not expect. I did not want the nostalgia back in my apartment. This new environment has power in it that I have never had before. I am baffled but glad.

In my car too were items for a new office look for my work as a writer. I have a set of nine clocks and a poster of the world to frame. It is my new global look to remind me of the reach i had already gained. I decided to retrieve them from the car. Before I did that, I put away the make shift folding furniture. I got the clocks from the car and put them on the wall in three rows of three, newscaster style. Then I put the poster of the world in a frame I had. All of them together signifying the top ten countries that my writing was read in. Only a few are what you would expect to find on such a display. When I was finished, something shifted in me. I am not sure what it means but it has so much power in it that I continued clearing nostalgia from my place and made a plan to replace items that are too worn to give all of it an upgrade.

 I started cleaning out the closet that had nostalgia in it. I knew that I knew that I needed to continue this sorting and cleaning. I had no idea that nostalgic items carry with them a link to the past and a heaviness. My place feels so much lighter. These nostalgic items included some things from my own past, things I bought from antique stores, and long past projects I will never do again. It looked crazy to throw out so many items that looked good. Even a worker at my apartments saw me carrying perfectly good looking stuff to the dumpster and told me not to. I smiled on the way there. He must have seen me working on it yesterday, why was I doing this? I don't know. I got my answer on the TV.

I tuned on the TV and found one of my favorite preachers on, John Gray. He said that it is "crazy praise" to do things that are contrary to what is going on. He gave a few examples. I was sure that this is what is going on with me. I am still getting pressure to stop writing, now from people I do not know as well as those who do. Some who have noticed how prolific I am. Others who are trying to understand why I am still doing this. The environment is not right here for what I do. When I woke up I heard someone screaming the F-word having an argument. Not a way I begin the morning, outside my window. I should be hunkered down in my apartment among the old and worn and out of date, swimming in nostalgia. Feeling sorry for myself. No, I am fixing it up and plan to stay one more year and said so yesterday to the manager who thought I was leaving. It is an example of "crazy praise".

 I have no budget at all for new furniture. Maybe I will get a few pieces to make it more comfortable for my stay here, somehow. I need a comfortable chair to write in, a living room group, a couple of barstools, and a bed. I know that it is a lot to ask for, and that I cannot go pick it up or lift it up to the second floor. Just the same, I am hoping. To get ready for this, I folded up the folding furniture I have and put it in the closet to make room for it. That is "crazy praise" too. It will help me to be still and let God fight my battles with my writing venture. A way will be made for this too. I feel better just looking at the clocks on the wall and planning the upgrade. It is a totally different style for me. I like it already. I am going classic ...that was once country, then feminine, then casual, then playfully artistic. Yeah, streamlined and minimal and classic are very new for me.

At this juncture, redecorating and upgrading my home is an act of defiance. Huh? Cutting loose of my old life is extremely threatening as is being open about things that I like and believe in. You know... like normal people do. Yes, like how my house looks matters to those who want to stop me. Huh? Exactly. I don't get it either.

So here I go, off on this lovely project to occupy me. It is going to be fun. I wonder how I will be able to get the items I need for it. I do have a little money, just not hundreds of dollars that it would normally take and the way to get it is closed to me right now.

The Self

I have heard it said that the home is a reflection on the self. It is not unusual for someone to want to remodel or redecorate when they are making changes within. Sometimes it is not that conscious. It is well known that late in pregnancy, women go through a "nesting phase" where all their attention is focused on the baby and getting their home ready for the infant's arrival. I did a lot of sewing during my first pregnancy and shopped more for the second as I was working. I know what it is like to experience nesting. Let me propose this: there are also other times of change in life stages that prompts this too, though it seems like someone just had enough of the old look, there could very well be things shifting in their perspective that prompted it.

For me, my house looked to worst when I was struggling with something. I would let things pile up and clutter to gather. I would not clean as well as I knew to. I would let too many things get old and worn. When I felt good, I would buy new items and try new things. These new items would replace some of the old. It was fun to try these things out. All the while, I would learn more about myself and shift the items in my house, getting to know myself a little bit at a time.

Since my last book, I have come to discover a few things I needed to change. As one who loves to bake and also diagnosed with prediabetes, I had to make a decision on the large collection of baking equipment I had. There will never be a time that I will be able to eat the treats I like to make, sad but true. It took me eight years to finally decide to let go of it all. Some of it I sold. I donated the cookbook collection to a community college. I threw the rest of it in the trash. Hard as it was, I no longer feel like I am missing something because objects are not there to remind me. Shifts like this in one's life are hard but adapting can happen and become a new normal. It is okay to make one's home reflect these changes.

For a little while, I thought my home should have my art and clothing designs on display. I have rethought that. The space was nice and large to make a show come together but I don't want to live in it. I would rather have a clean slate at home for new ideas to develop and not be influenced by what I have already done.

Introvert Environments

An introvert is a person who gets energy from being alone to recover their energy and regroup. Being with people depletes them and being alone for a time helps them to regain it. They prefer to do some things alone more than with large groups of people, sometimes. It is because such environments make them become depleted of their energy. They prefer small groups of people. They prefer talking about meaningful things over small talk. Parties are difficult for introverts because it involves lots of people and small talk, the two things that make an introvert uncomfortable and depleted. There is nothing wrong with being an introvert. It is an inborn thing. There is a lot to read on the topic. Making a home comfortable for someone with these preferences goes against the grain of the extroverts. Homes are even designed with the extrovert in mind with spaces for gathering and entertaining. The only solitary space in most homes is the bathroom. Or the study, if it has one.

As an introvert myself, this presents some unusual "problems" in decorating. The question is...how does one decorate in an environment designed for extroverts?

For the first time, I have a big space for myself, 800 square feet. I want it to be functional to the things I like and need to do. I have looked quite at lot of solitary spaces, called personal spaces. It is super cool what people do in these spaces, there are so many of them. I am certainly not alone with this idea. My space itself is almost an open concept. The living and dining areas are adjoining with the kitchen. The kitchen has an opening that has a bar on the other side of it. One can work in the kitchen without feeling secluded in there. The space has a vaulted ceiling in the living area, reaching about fifteen feet at the highest point. The kitchen and dining area has eight foot ceilings. The dining area has a mirrored wall on the top to thirds of the wall and wainscoting and painted paneling. The apartment has three closets with ample storage, not walk in but lots of space. The bathroom has a large vanity with one sink and counter space. The second section of the bathroom has the toilet and sink, which had a door to that area at one time. The bedroom is roomy with one of the closets filling the whole wall. There is a porch with railing that is balcony looking with its curved face and has a double sliding glass doors. The space features three more windows, one in the kitchen, one in the bathroom, and one in the bedroom.

I solved the problem this time by making the dining room into a study for my writing. I did not want a big emphasis on food and eating when I clearly cannot eat that much. The table becomes a place to dump stuff, like it used to be in other places I had. I like a gathering area in the living room for conversation and relaxing for when small groups of people come. No entertainment center. I am not big into media. No exercise equipment. Simple. Clean.

In my mind it is okay to use a room for different purpose than it was designed for. A home is a place to love to be in and take care of oneself. Introvert or extrovert, the space has a touch of the kind of person that lives there. It is not something to be ashamed of. It is okay to not like parties and big empty tables or even small ones. It is okay to have a reading corner and a place to work. I have a bar that is enough of a table for me, I rarely use. Now I will. I set up a tea kettle for having tea.

When considering when people come over, I have decided to not invite those who are critical. Who needs that? Not me. My home is for me. I am not going to invite people I will have to kick out. I just won't anymore.

Who I Would Become

In many environments I made for myself it was a statement of who I was at the moment I bought everything. Over time, I would simply outgrow it. This time the clocks idea had lead me to the idea of decorating for who I would become. How would I do that? The same place I got the clocks idea, in the quiet listening to the promptings of the holy spirit. Really? Yes. It matters to God that I look and feel my best and ready to fully take on the work that I have said yes to, his work for me.

I am to expand my "world look" throughout the house and do it all at once. I will be lead to where I will qualify for furniture, who will deliver it. Apparently I am to have some important visitors soon and need it.

I got to this answer from planning my environment. Day dreaming of the furniture I would love to have and praying too. I had it planned to every detail. I knew where to get the kitchen things at discounted prices. I knew I could make curtains and throw pillows on my sewing machine. I wanted something that would be a very strong statement and a strong contrast to the chocolate brown accent wall that is huge. I planned the art for the wall. All of it clean lined and a new classic kind of design. Then what happened was this: God said yes. Just like that when I chose teal as the accent color. There was just one change. Shelving instead of the fake fireplace.

I finally did it. I finally stepped away from the personal look of the quotes on the wall, lace, flowers, spiritual, and overtly feminine looks. I stepped away from the teenager gathering place my last furniture was. I finally stopped trying to prove I am creative. I finally took the emphasis off of food and put the focus on my work. I can't wait to see it all in place. It is neutral and not masculine, yet men may like it too. It is will suit the older style of the apartment which was built in the mid-1960s and upgraded a little by painting the paneling and the brick white. At least that was the plan.

"Lord you have searched my heart, you know when I sit and when I stand. All my ways are familiar."

Trip to the Store

Risk is okay in your head, it is another thing to walk in the store knowing full well once they know your reality, you could get tossed out on your ear. That's where I stood this morning when I went to the store directed to by God.

I found a salesman and we walked around with my list and I chose what I would buy, ten pieces of new furniture. I wanted to stop half way through. The word deep within said 'keep going'. I have never allowed myself to ever buy furniture like that. Ever. Now here I was doing so in old clothes with amazingly bad credit, following the holy spirit and trusting. It took two hours of crunching numbers, a discount, and two loans for me to get it all. Just like God had said. I was amazed. At one point I wanted to cry tears of joy. I have to return to get info back for the second loan when I have a phone number, of all things. It was the only thing stopping the whole deal from going through. The kindness and the care they put into it was amazing. They never once told me to put anything back or downgrade to something cheaper.

As I was leaving I went to check on one thing more, it was then I got a "we will work with you" and her story. I thanked her for the second chance and she said they do third and fourth ones too. She said, "Sometimes you just gotta have something beautiful for yourself". I teared up a little and agreed. I told her I was glad that this place was part of the process.

On the way out, I knew it was going to be tight to pay for it. I asked God about it. He said it would be paid off in a month. I thought about the beautiful things I had chosen and knew that it probably would be. How? I did not know. But I knew that God had sent me so many beautiful things already. He wanted me to trust him big and enjoy my home that he gave me for another year. The time it took for me to finish the plan I played with in my head the night before, and to buy the furniture was 4 hours. God does work like that.

"Even there your hand shall guide me, and your right hand hold me fast."

Nostalgia Items

Today I got the okay to bring up some nostalgia items from my car. God wanted me to put some on display in the built in. He particularly wanted me to put my ceramics I made on display. I made them at a community college years ago in a ceramic class. The one my parents enrolled me in when I wanted to quit high school. It was a class that saved me. The conditions were that if I went to high school all week, i could go to class on Saturday. I advanced through the classes, meeting and working with different instructors, from hand building to all the way through making myself a set of dishes on the potter's wheel. The classes saw me through high school, getting on the honor roll the last semester and through the community college to earning my associate degree. It gave me an opportunity to win a champion at the county fair which took me to the state fair.

As we were packing to go as a family to the state fair so I could exhibit, I took my ceramic piece out of its protective wrapping as to not forget it. Someone bumped the table and it crashed to the floor. Because of its construction, it broke only on one side and four square pieces fell out. I let out a cry. Everyone stopped. Are we still going? Someone asked. I looked at the four pieces and said yes. I glued it together with craft glue. I packed it and we left. When it was my turn before the judge, he was very kind. He said that it was a good pot and well-made but because it was broken and repaired, he could not give me the champion of the day. He gave me a blue ribbon. He said nobody would have done that. That was the stuff I was made of in those years. It is the same stuff I have returned to now, glad to be back. God was working back then too.

It took two days to put everything in place in my apartment. I threw out an amazing amount of stuff. Stuff that was not needed, like old paper work, and things that make strong emotions come up that I don't want to revisit anymore. I have less but it feels like more. More potential for the newness to come in, there is so much space for it to go.

I painted a picture frame black to match the others. I put artwork in them. I painted the name of the country each of the clocks represents on them. I cleaned and spent the day at home. I hadn't done that in a long while.

My Painting and My Sewing

I have been asking God in prayer to please not make me give up my painting and my sewing. I really wanted to keep these two things. As much as I love writing, I need a break from it sometimes. The painting is so relaxing for me. It is a lot of repetition in the kind of painting I do. A lot of tiny doodles that look like lace from a distance. My sewing has evolved to redesigning already made clothing. I love how fast it can go. I wanted to keep them both.

In the past, my creativity has been an all over the house activity. It was everywhere and got out of hand easily. In the house and family, I grew up in, it was okay. Out in the world, no. Yet in this new place in life that I was decorating for who I would become, I wondered if I would still love to do these two things in the future.

I got my answer.

I slept only a few hours and got up in the night. It was clear I was just going to lay there hoping for morning. Then I got the message to make the hall closet into a sewing center. I was to sort everything in the plastic bags I had and pin them up inside the closet. I loved the idea. I sorted the small equipment like the rippers and scissors. I sorted the thread and embroidery thread by color. Simple as it is, it honored what I loved. I hung a few projects. The closet is large enough to hold a sewing table. When I want to sew, I open the door and open the folding chair. I loved the simple idea that was not my own.

I asked about the painting. I would be in the other closet by the front door. I would not have done that before because I had other people in my house and it would block the coming and going of those that lived with me. In a place of my own it did not matter. I put all the Christmas stuff in the top of the closet and put my painting stuff in there. There was not much. I apparently get to go shopping for more painting things. This closet will hold a small table too. I can open the door and open the folding chair. I love that I can still do these things and contain them and have a regular house. I can leave things set up behind the doors.

I am so touched by all that is happening for me in this space. It is finally feeling like home.

Eating Area

I gave up my dining room to be my writing area, a kind of study or den. The activity of writing has no mess at all. I would eat at the bar. The furniture store would not let my buy any barstools unless it had a table. I thanked them for allowing me to get the big pieces of furniture. The industrial looking bar stools would have to go.

I was sent, like I am to often by the holy spirit, to go eat dinner out and to stop by the resale shop down the street. I was not sure I wanted to go. What did I find? A pair of bar stools so gently worn they looked new. They were better than the ones at the store and I got both of them for less than the price of one. They are wood and brown leather like fabric. They have a cushion on them and a back. The man at the store did not know if they would fit in my car. He said he could try before I bought them. They did. I paid and went home. They looked amazing.

Now I had some energy and went to the store and get some plates I had seen earlier in the day. I had wandered into the store next to the furniture store and looked at the color teal on things. I found some place mats to put on the bar. I felt prompted to get them. Now I had the color teal that would be the accent color in my home. I looked around at teal colored glass that was lighter in color and went beautifully with the place mats. Now I had another color to work with too. I looked around at dishes and then bought only the placements.

I was sitting on my new barstool and thinking about new glasses that went with the placements. The inner prompting told me the name of the store. I hadn't been there in a while. I went to look and yes there were plastic glasses that were that lighter color, big tumblers. I bought four. Then I was prompted to go and buy two plates. They are the kind you can buy how many you need, so I did. I got home and washed the dishes and put them in place. It looked amazing. I have a few more pieces to get to complete the area. It is just right for me and a friend who may come for lunch.

Getting Ready for the Big Furniture

I decided to get the place cleaned up after my cat died. Yes, he did in the process of writing this book and venture. I made a little memorial to him by painting on his food bowl, "In memory of Dani 2006-2017." He was almost eleven, just shy of his birthday. That made it easier to throw out his things and move on to taking good care of me by making the tiny memorial. I have that little reminder in the place he used to eat. I look forward to, to receive the new furniture.

There's the bedroom furniture, a bed and frame with headboard. It will be good to have something beautiful and not make shift, for the first time in my whole life. I was such a master of making things work. This time it is new and gorgeous.

The other big furniture is for the living room and the den. A couch and 2 chairs. A great big shelf. That pretty much fills the room.

The den has a chair and sofa table up against the wall. There are two ottomans that store things left over from my last studio. It put them close together near the kitchen to drop things down on them like groceries, when I bring them in.

The kitchen is galley style so there is no room for furniture.

It is an exciting time to be preparing a new environment for myself, very. It is going to be the best one yet and just for me.

Browsing

I went out and about today, wondering if I could get nice things I needed in my new color, teal. I stopped at two places. I was delighted with what I found. I could have replaced almost everything. I look forward to when I can. It really is more about letting go of the old than getting new things. Though the worn things look awful for sure, they are symbols of my old life. How I got them. How I wanted something else. About compromising to get something less than what I truly deserved. All that has to go, it is a good thing it is worn out.

What I am replacing them with are beautiful new things that sell from the department store merchandise that does not sell. They move it on to these outlet type shops. Everything looks amazing and once in your home with the tags off, no one would ever know you spent half price.

I saw herb blends in grinder containers, amazing scented soaps, pots and pan from cooking stores, towels, and bedding. I saw more teal colored items than I thought. It is that new a color for me. I just never noticed. It was fun to browse and dream.

I looked at items in a thrift shop to see what I might get for the accent pieces that pull a home together. It is a real departure for me to not choose what I did before. a more sophisticated look is on the horizon. That is way better than the looks I had before. It takes growing and changing to take on a new look regardless of what it is. My spaces were deeply personal. Now I can do that if I want in the closets where I will paint and sew I mentioned earlier. I looked for tables for these. There were none today. The thrift shops do have those large accent pieces like big glass containers that are out of reach full price. It will be good to add these pieces to the design of my home.

Unknown Items

Today I was sent to the hardware store and got paint chips. Fine by me only I will not be painting, my place is a rental. When I was there I chose all the teal colored paint chips and a booklet of one-day decorating projects to get ideas. There is something with these things I collected. I am not sure what. Kind of fun. Who knows what these are for?

Later in the evening, I went to see the kitchen things. I looked at pots and pans, mine are so old and awful looking. I was very surprised at all the choices. It had been a long time since I bought any. It is a hard choice. I also looked at toaster ovens. Some of them are toaster ovens and convection ovens, perfect for baking for one serving like I do. Very sleek and a cool idea. I never had a convection oven before. It bakes things faster and more efficiently than an oven and better than microwave. Things get browned and cooked evenly. It will be great to use these new items.

The color teal was everywhere. How did I not notice? There were pretty kitchen towels and glasses. There were laundry baskets and all kinds of teal things everywhere. It is probably a case of the more you notice, the more you get.

When I get to decorate with the help of the holy spirit, things get put together differently than I do and go in stages differently than I would. Unlike me, this will be done faster. Amazing. So many times in the past I would work on it so slowly that things would never look done and new all at one time. I think this is the first time. I love the simple design.

Days later, I found out that the paint chips were to help me select items for my home. I was to cut them apart and clip them together. I added the fabric samples of fabrics I had purchased. I could write on them which items I already had were that color on them. It was a surprisingly good idea, there are so many shades of teal out there that a guess could look terrible. I could take my color chips out and hold them to the item I wanted to check, making better choices.

Emerging Color

I have been feeling a little lost with this venture and could not figure out why. Yes, I was making an environment for who I was to become. That in itself could leave me feeling directionless without the holy spirit. It is a new thing for me to accept the idea that the holy spirit is very interested in my environment and all in the details. I knew for a long time what happens in the environment matters but color choices? Apparently so, much to my surprise. It does matter what I put in my new environment, a lot. Soon all the old will be tossed and the new will replace it. I love this starting over transition time.

My color choices have made some significant changes over time. My first teenage room was all neutrals, the monochromatic browns with an accent of orange, very 1970s and current at the time. My first apartment was neutrals with beige and a light blue accent. The bedroom had ruffles. Then I kept the neutrals and added slate blue and country accents like ducks and "welcome" written on things, very 1980s and trendy too. I took that accent color away and went with green leaves pattern on things in the 1990s, I wanted to bring the outside in. Then I moved and got a place that was all beige and bought beige furniture with jewel tone accents of forest green, gold, and cranberry in the 2000s. From there, I went back to the neutral browns like back in the 1970s with dark green and rust accent colors in the 2010s. I added white to that color palate for a bit of high contrast with dishes and lace, revisiting a feminine touch but not all over the house this time. Now It is the same brown neutrals with teal and white, a really bold and bright color scheme. The boldest ever, high contrast that pops.

A younger me would have not liked the bold contrasts at all but a relaxing neutral environment to calm my senses. It was a theme in my decorating. I have finally learned to calm myself and speak up. I am taking a stand on things important from me. Maybe that is the reason for the color changes. Teal is a blue green color with emphasis on the green. Green? It is such a surprise. Green has always appeared in my artwork in the form of a yellow green, from way back. Now it is back in a new way. It appears that my color choices have grown bolder over time as I have.

Furniture Buying 101

How does one go about buying furniture? As someone who has grown up in a large family, new furniture was for the living room. My parents bought furniture when we were little that lasted the lifetime of our childhoods. As I got older more and more siblings were born, second hand furniture was the norm. We all had what we needed but it was not trendy or new. I sat and slept on used furniture, that was in good condition to begin with. It was not stinky or worn or torn, it was just not new and nothing I would have chosen myself.

 I was in my forties with a new apartment with the need for furniture. I bought cots to make the transition for me and my kids. A few days in, we went furniture shopping at a warehouse in the back of the furniture store. It was there we chose the furniture together. I bought a couch, loveseat, and dinette set. The dinette set was a table and four chairs. That was a good choice, the fabric on the chairs was patterned and did not show dirt easily. The couches had a flaw I did not notice at the store, the seat cushions all worked their way to the floor. None of them were attached and even the smallest amount of movement would cause them to shift. Even visitors had to get up and rearrange where they sat. The background color was beige and showed dirt easily as it got to be the place backpacks were thrown and pet cats would sleep. I would do better next time.

Next time came with a move to larger quarters. I bought a five-piece sectional and ottoman. I had it treated to resist dirt. It was big and comfy. There was a flaw with it I did not notice. This time I had purchased furniture for tall people. My feet would not touch the floor when I sat on it or anyone else in my short family. It made for some awkward moments. The new dinette set was the taller cafe style. I chose the smaller table as I was thinking of my own future with no kids, they were growing up. The leather like covering on the chairs peeled. My little grandson peeled it and ate a few small bits. Most of it was retrieved from his mouth, thankfully.

Then on to having to leave with no furniture. I could not afford to bring it. It was eight months of folding furniture I could get in the car, some of it meant for outside. It broke quickly, I bought more, it broke too. There was no chance for furniture until God stepped in, when I let go and let him have control.

I think my choices are better. Can't wait for delivery. Over the years, I came to measure the spaces, as I had purchased a few pieces that did not fit. I bought furniture to suit the space. It worked out better and I did not want to move the old furniture. I finally had the confidence to lay down on a bed in the store. I actually bought on without doing so and bought too firm a mattress years before. I had matched the label with one I had but the one I had, had softened over time and it was not the same as new.

Furniture buying, like anything else needs practice to know what you like and how your will care for it. I did buy smaller pieces to paint and suit my space. I did buy put together furniture, not my strength. I did not have the proper tools. I also bought the kind where if you make a mistake, it is locked in place and you cannot change it. I had to put up with backwards pieces.

So now you know why this is such a big deal for me. It is me with better than I knew to do coming in the truck in a few days, thanks to the holy spirit. Rather exciting.

Not knowing What I like

Quite a lot of people do not know what they like and cannot decide on a color palate or style or anything. I was like that too. For me, it was because I did not know myself. Plain and simple as that. It was years of..."this is so you", that wasn't so much. My "this is so you" changed from person to person and year after year. I had to find out. An interior designer on TV had the answer, buy magazines and tear out the things you like and put them in a folder. I did that. Now what?

I did not know, I saved the folder. With the help of Sarah Ban Breathnach and her <u>Illustrated Discovery Journal</u>, i learned to interpret what I had. Her book now out of print, boiled down to this: get in a relaxed state when you select the pictures. When finished collecting, then look for patterns. What do you see? When I look for patterns, I move things around and put them in groups, sorting them into my own categories. I took out the folder and there it was neutrals with lots of textures. That idea has pretty much stuck with me my entire adult life and in the environments i have built for myself. Even before I realized there was a pattern, it was there in my choices.

So there you go, a process just for you. It is truly a lightbulb moment for me that was great to experience. It made clothes buying easier, making choices easier, and my decorating easier. It was because the choices were narrowed considerably. Browsing went faster. Shopping went faster. I had fewer clothes in my closet and objects I did not like by having this information.

Pay particular attention to the colors you do not like too. It is possible that there are some shades you do like of that color. I found I did not like yellow ochre at all. I would never decorate with it or wear it. What I found was my favorite shade of beige is a very light shade of ochre! It was the ochre that gave it the glow I liked. Another color I do not like is kelly green, a little too "leprechaunish" for me. Yet, my new color is teal, that very color with blue in it. Who knew? Preferences can be so deceiving.

Window Treatments

Today I am making the window treatments out of the fabric that I have, that lovely bight teal color that pops. I want to allow as much of the natural light to come in as possible in my home and still give the place a finished look. It is a color that a little bit can go a long way.

The furniture has not arrived yet so there is lots of space to work and put up the window treatments. The only room that is going to have full curtains is the bedroom, a little darker is okay there. The color gives a nice glow when the sun comes up too.

The kitchen and the bathroom will have a simple valance of one triangle point. These will be hung at the top with push pins or tacks. As a renter I need to be considerate of the space I am using to not drill holes in the walls and attach curtain rods. It would cost me later to have them filled. Push pins and thumb tacks hang things securely and leaves a very small hole that can be painted over easily later.

That will be pretty much it for the window treatments for today. I want to do something more with the glass wall of mirror that is in the dining room turned study and the sliding glass door that leads to the patio balcony. That is for another day.

Furniture Delivery Day

I was excited about the furniture coming. I woke up early as usual. I wandered about the store looking at the things I had picked out the other day. I went home with a few groceries an hour later.

Then I got my home ready for furniture, I swept the porch and arranged things. I wasn't sure what time the furniture would come. I ate and then was instructed to praise God. I put on "Godspell" and added singing and dancing to the praise session, happy and excited. Not knowing the delivery time, I missed it. I went to the store. They gave me a phone number to reschedule.

When I got home, my phone would not work. I had it only a few days and got some annoying texts and let the battery die. I was so disappointed. I took a nap. I got up and felt terrible still. I decided to do some crazy praise and sew a garment for the book I am working on the same time as this one, Altered Couture: maternity wear. I stitched the top that I cut out yesterday, It turned out cute and is the first garment in the book. That is crazy praise.

I decided that I needed to do more praise instead of feeling sorry for myself. I needed to keep going. I needed to trust God that his blessing would find me and not the others.

I got to thinking about the TV preachers I watched today. Bishop TD Jakes had a great message. He talked about how both the past and the present were both pulling at him from either direction. He had two men come up and pull on each arm as he talked. He then freed himself from the past and let the future move him on. He talked about how people do not believe that you are changed, they only see what they knew of you from the past. So this is the struggle I face today. Disappointed that the past is still pulling me back.

Another preacher, that is new to me talked about why dogs bark when you walk by. It is because you are going somewhere and they are not. People are like that too. They do not like to see you moving forward without them. So they "bark" to keep you where you are. He also said that people will put you in a box and expect for you to live like they want you to but when you put them in a box, they won't do it.

I love these TV preachers. They help so much. I have to keep believing in the freedom I have and not let this setback bother me. Who knows? It could come tomorrow. It will be okay. It will.

"Your rod and your staff hold me up, lest I dash my foot against a stone."

Whole and Beautiful

My living environments have always been make shift or incomplete. I was not affected by that, or so I thought. I accepted it. This time God has shown his promise by giving me the opportunity to have a new and finished environment to live in. That has to be something that will affect my new work and life. He made a way at a time in my life where it looked the least possible to do. It feels unbelievable.

It is a process too. All of this is going to be put in place. Although it is new, it reflects my new simple living that I came upon and developed for me to eat healthy. I have been wondering if this book is a yellow cover book, one to help those in need. I think it does. It is for those who are poor in spirit too, a kind of inner poverty that one might have regardless of income. Like me. Having evidence of being poor in spirit is all around those who build environments that are stuck in the past or where the present quickly becomes the past. This is a new approach for me is worth spreading.

Interior design works from finding out who one is and builds the environment accordingly. They have good ideas about placement of items in the environment. This idea would be a reach for them. Interestingly enough, it is not so far a reach in style that it makes me uncomfortable either. That would be easy to do. I am not sure it is even possible to do without the hand of God directing it and the holy spirit giving inspiration. I don't. It is a reach into the unknown that no one person can know.

Browsing Again

This morning I went on another trip about town to browse. I looked at the part of the store I went to yesterday. I looked at several other things before I came upon the comforter I would get for my new bed. I nearly cried when I saw it. It was so beautiful and sophisticated and luxurious. It was not the one I had picked out a few minutes before. God does not like it when I take over, thinking I know what comes next. I was way off in guessing what he had for me. I love this new look. He is most definitely concerned about the details. It matters very much to him how my environment is going to look and feel. Even though he is my father in heaven, he is not like an earthly man that I think he is. No, I was formed in his image too. My femaleness is part of him too and the things I like to do and am concerned about. He doesn't have to scratch his head and wonder like an earthly man does about what I like. He fully gets it.

Something else I found was a source for more fabric. It is exactly the same color and cheaper, less than half the price. I am scratching my head on this one too. I do not know why I was sent to the other place and got that fabric for curtains. I did have a conversation with someone about paring the bright teal with chocolate brown. She was amazed an old lady like me would chose that color and was surprised and delighted.

I am going to hesitate more before I do something when the directions are not clear. I simply cannot decorate for who I will become without him. That's the whole point. He wants me to need him in everything.

Reason for the Help

I have discovered that the reason I am getting so much spiritual guidance is that it is part of managing the grieving process over my old life and losses I have endured the past two years or so. It is a chance to heal. Losing everything is no small thing plus two people and my cat. A new fresh environment is how this new life begins for me. It has to, I simply cannot live without the comforts of real furniture, not folding and new towels, not old. It would be a less than environment to continue that way, not good. It is a process that is a labor of love I cannot resist. I love to do this, even though the grief. The spiritual help narrows the choices and helps me to decide. It introduces new ideas that I would not be able to do in this state.

It is becoming more apparent to me that I should not be able to do this after so much loss. I have been observing myself and fumbling on the small stuff but writing, sewing, and painting...no. No trouble at all. Things like writing down my address, yes. Taking a wrong turn to someplace I know well...yes. I should not be able to make decisions for this venture, I should not.

They say that God is in the details. I honestly thought to the contrary. But it is amazingly true. More details than I can imagine. He is the ultimate in micromanagement that I so need right now. The place is going to be beautiful.

Crazy Praise Again

I got the new furniture delivery dates. It is coming in two batches. It is a straightforward process that is no big deal...set the date, they call and give the window of time for delivery to be home. Then I confirm. On delivery day, they call again when they are on their way. It is only four steps but it can be amazingly complicated when things are going as they are for me. It is the unseen things that have been blocking what I need... traffic, weather, phone signal problems. It is unreal how easily something like this can be stopped or interrupted. And it has to happen twice. I keep trying, with the idea of crazy praise on my mind. It is a relief to be decorating in the midst of this.

I heard a TV preacher put it like this, codependence does not like change and will not allow it, it feeds on the awfulness that keeps it going. Another TV preacher beside her, Joyce Myer said that "any relationship that does not affect you for some reason to be there, will infect you when it is time to leave". There are negative consequences to staying that I saw a long time ago. I know that I am free. The regular take downs are getting more intense but farther and farther apart. I sense in my spirit that I am and will be safe the entire time I do this.

Another Browsing Trip

I went on another browsing trip today to a local home decorating store. They have middle range items for the home, not just plastic but nice things too. Plastic is there too if you want it. I went straight for the pillows for the living room. There were so many there. Finding something that would go with this new look of mine was hard at first. Then I remembered I was going to make them. It was still easier looking in the blue aisle. It was too easy to find what I used to choose and still like. Then I found one of those rose petal pillows of soft fabric that looks like a giant flower and feels wonderfully silky. It was for the bedroom. Oh...the bedroom. I liked it. It was a nod to the feminine decorating style I had a while back. It will look great against the teal comforter in beige.

Another nod to my feminine side I found in the bathroom aisle. The shower curtain hooks had glass diamond like decorations in clear on them. A little like those old time door handles. I am making the shower curtain and putting it up anyway for color without the liner, the bath girl that I am. It looks like something is missing without it. I had trouble matching the color of teal to the carpets. How about white? I had white before. Try a new texture. Then i found something I liked, new for me. I found a hand towel rack, very pretty, like jewelry for the bathroom.

Then the kitchen aisle I found the really nice quality but not expensive kitchen tools in shiny chrome. Heavy in weight, would last a while. Very classic. No teal colored funky stuff for me. Yeah, now you're getting it, I felt the encouragement. I realized too if I put too much teal in my place it would no longer be an accent color anymore. I found teal canisters with black lids that matched the curtain fabric. They had chalkboard paint to write the contents on the outside with chalk, cute and a bit of a nod to teaching. I loved the clear small milk bottles like the ones i drank milk out of in first grade. I thought no but got a yes. Amazing. The little case of them is a nod to the nostalgia I like so much. they come with straws too. Cute to put on the counter. I found an easy to hang paper towel holder and a trash can. Yep, I would need those too.

I didn't get any of the stuff, it helped to learn to recognize my new classic style that will be me as I grow into it. I look forward to the day I can get items like this. I love the little nods to my old styles, it personalizes it without over taking the place like I used to let it do. Hummm, I am really catching on to something.

When I got home, I was thinking about the bathroom curtains being too short and not liking that at all. I was told to make some quilting points out of the remaining fabric. Quilt points? I hadn't thought if those in a long time. It was part of my country style. I had made a pillow out of them like more than twenty years ago. That had to be the holy spirit on that one, for sure. It looks amazing. I put the window treatment up. Who is this new woman emerging? She sure has fire in her, I thought looking at the finished windows. I had the idea to add them to the shower curtain I was making to carry the theme a little further. I was told I would use them in the kitchen too, but not on towels. Who knows where that will be...this is fun to do and to sleuth out and to take one step at a time. I like it so much.

The Bridge

I have been thinking quite a lot about isolation, something they cautioned us against at a grieving support group meeting. I know I am not isolating; I am just not in touch with those who are against me living a life completely of my own choosing. It appears to look like I am isolating because I have so few bridges, something I was not encouraged to do in my old life. There have been take downs after take downs. I should not be able to stand up or function after so much of it. Just the same I am grieving the loss of the familiar.

I saw an interesting story on the news about a bridge between North Korea and China. It is how they get supplies into the "most isolated country on earth." It is a single freight bridge that has an older smaller bridge beside it. It is heavily controlled by China. When I saw that, the war of words between the two leaders didn't scare me anymore. China could very easily become the peace maker in the situation by stopping all shipments of supplies to the bridge. It would also be an easy bridge to take out, made of iron girders. The results to their country would be catastrophic.

I think about that bridge this morning and the idea of isolation. Whether it is a small group of people or a country built on fear and isolating, the results are the same. The bridges to the outside are much too few to be counted on for long periods to time. It is a precarious position to be in. I did not realize that at first when I fully left. I knew I would be alone for a while. I went out and about every day. I have been visible in the community for small things like having tea and shopping. These are small bridges but more of them.

When I got the message to go and buy furniture, I found some really cool people that are supportive of my new life. I found great people in unexpected places. I found what is now my new church, who is helping me heal. The bridges are getting bigger. They are getting more plentiful. The news of my story is unusual to them but they are curious. This is good. I am to prepare my new environment now because I will be busy soon. The flimsy bridges in my life had to be taken down in order for the strong ones to be built. It was scary.

I think about anyone who is reading this book that might be isolating. My thoughts are this: you can make it as pretty as you want but in the long run if it is a place to isolate in, it will not be right. There is a huge difference between being an introvert and isolating that not many see. The introvert has connections, healthy ones. Their home is a retreat to regroup. Those that isolate have few to no connections to the outside. Their home is not a fun place to be in, more like a jail of their own making. Feeling trapped at first, I did not know what to do without these few places I had that did not feel safe to go to. My mind was a little like North Korea that way. With the help of the holy spirit I ventured out and found multiple places to conduct the same business of food shopping and the like. My tiny circle is much larger. I meet so many kind people out and about. It gives me hope and I don't use those old bridges like I used to, but many of them with a sense of adventure and not seclusion. I am not going down, though North Korea might.

My hope though, is that China steps in like the holy spirit did for me with a solution that is loving. We both, world leaders and I, have the opportunity to take an aggressive stance in these parallel instances. I chose the longer path to follow God's lead. It has lead me to not bother with them and continue building my own future. That is the stronger stance. It gives me hope and new fulfilling work that I am piecing together as I heal. Something much too strong and too widely disseminated to take down by having only a single bridge.

Environments Matter Revisited

Although I know that the environments where I live and grow matter and quite a lot, it is hard to recognize and build one that is right for me without God's help. It is one for me that I cannot see for myself. Try as I might, I just do not know. My situation feels so touchy on one hand so new on the other. People like me are seen as different for sure and are thought to have needs different from the regular folks. What I found the truth is that we are all more alike than different. We meet the struggles of life in a different way, we are forced to be innovative far beyond what others have to do. Seen as stupid sometimes, that is not the problem at all. Degree or no, we just haven't found the right environment for our extraordinary insights and innovative way we have to live. Few open their doors to such a dilemma. I have had numerous ones closed to me and others not even opened. There are literal locked doors everywhere that are not open in either their physical doors or minds. Even if I have gotten in, the request is quickly rejected. It has been a long journey to find the patient people I have.

I was even considering and planning a long trip in an RV, not to just see the country but restore my faith that there were still good people in the world. Like everything else good, this too was walking distance from my home in my "100 foot rule" that I discovered 6 years ago. Yes, what I needed was indeed right close at hand. It is very hard to find when all of the area is so familiar.

That's the thing when creating an environment that is just right, what we think we need might not be. That is where God comes in. I love that he cares that much to guide and help me build mine one step at a time. I would not have chosen this, but now that I am getting it, I am learning to love both the approach to it and the results I am getting.

We different people are seen as out of focus and out of control but the truth is, it can get downright panicky when there is no place to go and get needs met by people who "get it". It can become an emergency quickly as the resources are fewer for us and the choices are made for us that don't need to be. There are more penalties. It can make us angry and awful to be with. But that is not who we are. We are not our diagnoses or our past. We are people without a place. That is all it is. Something pretty easy to supply...a sense of belonging and the opportunity to not to have to pretend what we have been through. I found that being surrounded by kind, loving, patient people I learned to relax enough to hear the promptings of God more and settle into his mighty arms. It was a place I did not know I could go for comfort. It is there I found the people who have also found the same. That has made the difference to me.

Environment that has furniture is a good thing, I will not turn it away. But to have a sense of place and belonging too is what I had hoped for with it. It is the very thing middle and upper income folks buy when they buy a home. It comes with it. In marginal and low incomes, there is no such thing. Lost and alone comes with that in ways that would horrify those who have never experienced it.

As one who can cross back and forth between the marginal and middle class lives, I think I know. I am building a bridge of understanding in a place few have done before. I hear the assumptions back and forth but no one has actually talked to each other. The marginal and the low income see it as a money problem, if they had more... life would be good. The middle and upper income see it as an annoyance and a blight to the community. They also possess the poverty of the spirit I mentioned earlier, that of boredom and loneliness with no real direction to their lives. What we all are is human beings, each with a different need missing regardless of income. It is not a money problem at all but a difference in perspective, need, and unusual rules that build walls rather than bridges. Let this be a bridge.

The Church as Refuge

While I was following God and all his many steps in this process, I found refuge in the church. When I was frightened, I would go there simply because the doors were opened early. They had no problem with me sitting on the chairs and resting in one of two areas for visiting used before and after services with free coffee, tea, and wifi. I nearly fell asleep once or twice. It was good to be in God's house. I would listen to music that was practicing in the church and enjoy being greeted by the people who work there. It was a place that had people, during a lonely time for me. It was at first, one of my many places I went to feel safe. Now it is my go to place, almost always open.

It is nice that God's house is still a refuge in some churches. That the doors are always open. I love this about my new church. I wish the others would take the locks off and greet people too. Their fear might really be their gift, if they let it go. Someone like me in all a tither could come in and calm down and show their gifts and talents. It could be a bold move for some to have to listen and meet people without appointments. I know a church is not an emergency room but it was for me. I loved how they responded. I hope I will be there a long time to come.

The fear in society need not be there to the degree it is. Faith and community are insulation from things like that. Young people are leaving church like mad, not knowing that they are losing more than they know. Short sightedness is part of the teenage and young adult years. Open churches could be a place to come and just be, to figure things out and feel safe. I know it sounds like days of old in a modern society. People living in a church to escape the world. One need not live there to reap the benefits of its safety, love, and caring. My hope is that more churches would open their doors again like when I was a child.

You could walk into any church at any time, sit down and contemplate things. This was long before the coffee shop like additions were added. Now it is more welcoming than ever. It is my kind of environment that suits so many, their parking lot is not quite big enough at times on Sunday. It is a place to come early and stay late. God's house should be more like that in other places.

Why it Matters

Letting God lead in building a new environment is essential. Why? Because without his attention to details it would be **too easy to build the same environment again** somewhere else. People do it all the time. They build what they know. I would too without the directions I got. I do not need a replica of what I have walked away from.

This is a great relief to me. It helps me be assured that this really truly is a new life for me. I like how God puts little nods of my past in it too, as to honor and not truly forget my old styles and memories of the good that happened along the way. I know too that his lead makes it fun and a surprise at every step. It is an adventure to see who this new me that is coming as the broken me is grappling with the scars.

I would hope too that others take God up on it. It was him that wanted me to write it in this book for you. to give you an idea of what is possible. I know that your journey will be surprisingly different, good different.

I close this section of my book with this idea so it will stand out to you and cause you to think. As for me, the furniture is coming tomorrow! I cannot wait. I am so excited. I have shopping to do to replace the old and add the new I never thought about.

As for it looking so straightforward? It wasn't. I took so many wrong turns and risked so much. If you decide to do this, you can expect confusion and all kinds of things to stop you or try to. If you choose not to stop, God will give you the kind of help you need when you need it.

***

Part 2: Before and After

Before...

I felt so embarrassed and shame for not having what I needed...
like furniture. It was the worst make shift place I ever had. I am
surprised I put up with it for so long. Sometimes it is a notion
that we deserve it when such things to happen. It is a horrible
cycle to get in, in your mind. It is terrible to get stuck in it. I
looked the place after I had thrown out a few broken chairs and
started to fix it up. The emptiness bothered me almost as much
as the folding furniture. I really believed I had no choice. It is
easy to think that. It was the kind of thinking that others placed
on me. Who is this woman who claims to have a master's
degree? If she is not lying, then how stupid is she to walk away
from an opportunity like she had? Everyone has their story on
how things went bad in their lives and encounter blame and
more shame instead of help. Following the urgings and the holy
spirt worked with that too. God does not want me stuck in that
place or anyone else for that matter.

"You who dwell in the shelter of the Lord, who abide in his
shadow for life, say to the lord my refuge, my rock in whom I
trust."

During...

They moved in the first group of furniture yesterday. After the delivery men left, I started arranging and taking out stuff. I put my TV on the shelf and plugged in it. A song on the Hillsong channel said...God can move mountains came on. I was very touched. I discovered too that the few things I do have to put on the shelf, I don't want them there. It has been another major shift.

I also put up a few pieces of my art with the clocks too. The den is nearly done. It is all so different for me. It is hard to know what to do with the gift of this opportunity and blessing. I opened a little book they gave me at church, it said that God was going to give me more blessings. This one is so overwhelming. It is hard to imagine more.

A few days later, I went on a shopping trip to get some items for my home. It was scary. I had been beaten down so badly by life that I found it hard to go get them. It turned out that all those browsing trips made it go fast. I have bedding and new pots and pans. I have so many other things I picked up today too. It took a good while to put them in place. I feel like I am coming back to middle class instead of living in the margin of almost and not quite. There is a huge difference, really huge. It is beyond words to know how good it feels. Though it was two years, it was really longer than that. It is almost my whole life of almost and second best. i had no idea God cared so much for me, his love beyond measure. People can be so flippant how they use these same words and not really know.

I am throwing away the items the new ones replaced. It is hard to stop using them. New items were always for guests and special occasions. That is how I grew up. Then the old items were saved and used until they were unusable and became trash. The really nice items were rarely used. This went for everything including clothes. This is a real stretch outside my comfort zone that I have never experienced before. It makes me think of the Chinese idea of "chi".

Chi is the energy in the room. Old things have little to no energy. They become stagnant. Stagnant chi is bad; it does not allow for growth. I realize that with new items of things I really need, there is almost no stagnant chi at all in my place. Things like glass make for active chi. Too much glass in the bedroom can make it hard to sleep, thankfully there is no glass in the bedroom except for the window that will have drapes. I have almost a whole wall of mirror in the dining room turned into the den. It is the perfect place to work with energy moving. It is the room I need the most energy. It is good I do not eat in there as it was designed.

It is really amazing how little I really need and now that almost all of it is new, I think I am on to something. It matters not one flip that there is nothing in the cupboards. Everything i need is out and available to use. I love this simple living with beauty in it. It does not have to be ugly or camping items to be simple living, who knew? Not me.

It took me about five days to get used to my new bed, it felt so different than the cot. The aches and pains from sleeping on make shift furniture is gone. Today I remembered when Corrie Ten Boom was freed from the concentration camp the first thing she got to experience was clean white bedding. It seemed like a miracle for her to be dressed and sleep in the hospital bed. I have a similar thankfulness. The joy of new clean sheets is something I will never take for granted again. It has been two years since I slept in a bed with sheets that was my own.

I made a window valance for the bedroom out of the pillow shams and hung it up. It looks so good with the antique crystal hanging from it that I had in my stuff, a touch of something I used to do often...go antiquing. I look forward to the getting the panel to hang under it to complete the window.

The black writing chair is amazing too. I was to choose a "power" chair, like one might have in an office. I can sit in it with an ottoman I had or with my legs folded it is so wide. I have written another book already.

Tropical Storm Harvey

I had no idea there was going to be a storm in the middle of this project. Although Harvey was a full blown hurricane in Corpus Christi, TX, where I live in Houston it was a tropical storm. The outer bands pounding rain now and again. It is projected to follow a cool front after landfall and the remnants of Harvey the hurricane will come here for what officials called a "rain event" and nothing to evacuate for. It is impossible for them to predict how much rain will fall and where in an area so large and relatively flat. The predictions vary from 12 inches to 36 inches of rain. Though we do have large, deep bayous to carry the water to Galveston Bay, sometimes the rate at which it falls is too fast for it to run off, four or five inches can flood streets and make then impassible if it comes in a very short time. This happens every now and again even without a named storm. What we did not expect was 50+ inches of rain, 51 inches in my part of town.

The Forecast of Fear

The news reports are very graphic the way describing the damage and filming the tops of submerged cars, with no bodies visible in them. It creates and environment of fear coming through the television, spreading the fear far and wide. Because of these prior events, fear can be seen at the grocery stores. There always seems to be a run on bottled water, canned goods, and dry goods that can be eaten without cooking. In Texas, price gauging is illegal, to charge more than they normally would for essential items in preparation for the storm. The fear running so high on the TV last night that there were several accusations of price gauging that were not, a reporter running all over the area to check them out.

This is not the kind of environment that is good for people. Few seem to be sensitive to what this fear is doing to them when the directions are simple...prepare and then do not go anywhere. People with resources leave very early to places far or another home out of town to ride it out. People without resources have another story to tell.

In all flooding and storms, there is the vulnerable population that the leaders work hard for. They are those without resources to leave or the physical ability to leave. These folks become trapped in their homes and have to be rescued. Some die. In this rain event, I am one of these in the vulnerable population. God in his infinite power had me doing wonderful things with my resources for sure this month and saw to it I had hardly any food or gas and no money to do anything to prepare for it. The rain event is supposed to be over the day I get paid.

I made a few calls for food and there were no centers giving out food in preparation of the storm. I got really scared. All I had was my faith to keep me company and my God, exactly what those in the vulnerable population have. I could not understand why there was no distribution of supplies anywhere. Perhaps this happens after the fact when the Red Cross comes in and brings the MREs, meals ready to eat, the same ones they give to the military. I saw this after hurricane Ike. No one was getting anything to take home, they were to accept the precarious position of getting help meal by meal. I did not want to be in that position. Now I think I am.

<u>My Reality</u>

This storm, my faith has lead me to something new as I was filled with fear from the TV, to let Jesus comfort me in my fear. It was something I had never done before. I found myself visualizing the foot of the cross in my mind's eye looking up at Jesus feet. As I imagined, a few drops of his blood fell on me, the hunger from eating such small meals left me. He had filled me with himself. I was to continue to do so and promised the other things that bother me would leave too.

It was a restless night. I did sleep but found myself with a discomfort that was not hunger, things like worry and restlessness, moving around more than usual in my bed. I was fighting something, though not sure what. I am going to have a new environment inside me when it is over. It is a huge trust walk for me with Jesus. I am beginning to understand my Easter message I got, "will I still be your superman, (when this is over)?", it is that intense. The scripture "Lord, to whom shall I go?" comes as an answer right now. There is no one to help but him. My inner environment matters to him, a lot.

The sun has risen for the day. Another band of rain is coming through. I opened up my front door and looked at the creek about 50 feet away. It has risen in the night. The people in the buildings closest to it getting more vulnerable by the hour, provisions or not, to flooding. My heart going out to them, as I look. For the first time I do not feel lucky to be on the second floor and a few feet further away. Nope, my inner environment is changing already. I want to help but with what I do not know. We are all powerless to this storm in various ways.

I was directed to turn on the TV and found uncertainty. They are working hard to try and project where the storm will go. Some say west, away from me, some say east directly to me, another says it will go south and then north. They just don't know. I talked with a neighbor earlier and she is not concerned although she went down to the creek to see. She said it was not bad. Others in the area said it was not bad in other storms either. I do not know what to think.

I think more about my inner environment, trying not to overwhelm myself with the strange set of possibilities that will probably not happen, the fear of running out of food and the like. No, I remember days of chaos and feeling better when something like this happened, taking me away from the life I hated for a few days. It did not matter if it was a storm or a sick child or a planned day away, I felt better away from life as I knew it and the expectations of others. I could not wait for the next emergency. Now, my inner environment is trying to heal from it. I fear sometimes, the uncertainty of every day being unpredictable of its content to be like a storm I carry around reacting to the uncertainty. Jesus wants to heal that. I want it too, a routine to follow and something predictable would be good. Yet I know I will keep changing it, if the storm in me is not healed. This is my opportunity.

I look around too at the environment of my apartment that is not finished yet. The teal color soothing to my eyes. I am getting used to the idea that this is me now or will be soon. It will for sure when the inner storm is over. It is interesting how God coordinated it with the actual one outside my windows. This inner storm has no clean up like the one outside will, no it is cleaning up in the midst of the outward one. It could not happen in calm. It doesn't work that way.

I have no idea why I needed to even buy furniture or do many of the things I have except that it makes me learn things about myself and trust God more. That is reason enough, I suppose, to soften my hard exterior of the scarring that has built up layers over the years, meant to protect me but actually keeps me away from what I need most. Kind people. I think this new softer me who is not so ready to fight at the slightest "wrong" move that probably isn't, calming my hurricane within for the promise of the glimpse. Only by grace will it happen, and I am never alone. It was a glimpse of what was to come, given to me six years ago.

It was a rough night, really rough. The storm was moving so slowly that the rain event turned into massive flooding. I was woken in the night about 1am. Neighbors on the first floor went into a panic as water came into their apartment, four young men who did not speak English well. They let themselves out of a window. The yelling and the trying to bail water was frightening. They pounded on doors of other neighbors, but not mine. I was so frightened I huddled in my bed. Colored lights flashed in my room. Then there was no more yelling, apparently they left. I finally fell asleep about 5:30am after doing yoga. The tenseness of the night made my body ache and I was trying to relieve it. It turned out one had injured himself and went to the hospital.

Mid-morning, the news brings tales of people cutting holes in their roofs to be rescued. There are rescues of all kinds with boats of all sizes from kayaks to air boats. The area was unprepared for this much water. They are calling it an historic event, breaking all the records. The newscasters are exhausted and cannot leave, some on the air for more than 12 hours. "Who's counting," one quips "we came to do this kind of work as a service to people."

All the while the holy spirit instructing me to hold on to God. I would not lose electric power. It flashed only once and came back on. The building across the way is dark. My needs look small compared to others in the area. Everything is dry. Helicopters have been flying over where I live, it is the coast guard looking for and transporting people.

What has happened to this project? I am learning more about environments than ever before as I sit and wait through a storm no one can stop. I am one of the lucky ones. Environments matter. It matters that one keeps their eyes on God and listens to the directions he gives. They are there for everyone who will listen. It matters to trust God in everything big or small. It just does.

 I cannot grasp the why of the extreme loss. Some rescued from second floor of townhouses, not wanting to stay. I cannot comprehend the idea of a vengeful God. Though he let my loss teach me. Perhaps there is something good in it for others too as this big city of 17,000 square miles rebuilds such large areas, America's fourth largest city.

<u>Quiet Came</u>

It was the third night of the storm; the rain had lessened in the night. The newscasters' hopeful that the eye will come over us soon. It is the place of calm as it passes through. A lot of the heavy rain is now to the east of the city. It was a quiet night. All the picture taking of the flooded creek beside the property has given way to quiet, the party atmosphere subsided, easy to do when one does not have to report for work. The rain is steady but not torrential, like a rainy day.

The sleep has done me good. There is a calm about me too. I found comfort in the psalms of the bible yesterday especially psalm 29, speaking to me and include storms, floods, and naysayers talking badly. I saw on TV too that the people outside the area are poised to come help us. There is a large line of 18 wheelers from HEB, a grocery store chain waiting outside of town to help, some that say 'disaster relief' on the side. There is a peace about me today that all will be well. My inner environment is trusting God softly and not with white knuckles as before.

It is raining hard again. They have talked about this being a 500 year storm, then an 800 year storm. It is an expression in both cases, the records do not go back that far. It helps with trying to figure the probability of it happening as unbelievable as it is...it was way less than .2% by now what contracts call an "act of God" that they cannot predict. There is a swath of dry air getting bigger and looking a little like the hand of God himself but not much. It is what my hope is based on as it looks to be scooping the storm away. The eye will arrive soon.

Purpose: to build on Love

My work as a writer has been taking a new direction to help people through it with information on simple living and trusting God. Now the direction of rebuilding comes into play, something I am doing myself. This could be good... to be just a little ahead of so many, new to having to rebuild what the flood and wind has ruined or any storm for that matter. On the TV yesterday was an interview of an older man moved to tears at the possibility of have to rebuild, again. It is hard work. He is tired and weary of it all. I get it. It is even harder with someone on your heels that takes it down as fast as you can get it up. I get the weariness after a storm that has destroyed everything. I get the not wanting to rebuild, but to be whole and healthy people we must. We must walk into the future with confidence that love will meet us there. It is my hope anyway. I have evidence of it like the outer bands of it reaching my soul already with drizzles of kindness that are so welcome in a parched life like my own, one that has been devoid of it for some time. I accepted the copy instead of the real deal. Yes, even love has copies. I will never do that again. I will continue to build this new life for myself. The truck will come. It will.

It is amazing what people will do when the rain stops temporarily. They get out in their cars out of curiosity and to be with family. I love the love that drives it. No matter how bad the weather and the forecast gets, there is always someone on the Transtar cameras, that film the roadways in real time. The newscasters are rotating their outfits pulling marathon long hours of work for us. I have been watching it that long. The rescues are still happening. Those that can help are coming out in droves with food, fuel for police boats, and dry clothes. The loss is extreme. I wonder how my meager account of this disaster will help. It will. In faith I know it will, though not known to me.

<u>Fear Comes Back</u>

I remembered the stench after hurricane Ike the day they opened Galveston up to visitors. It was something I never smelled before or since. Maybe even the smell of death mixed with mold and garbage. I start to cry, feeling hopeless.

'Keep your eyes on me.' I hear inside of me.

I know that in order to fix the city, it will go further than all the resources it has, others will rise up. Others like me with expertise. Others with strengths and talents to rebuild that no one knows about. After the terrorists of September 11th, my then professional organization that I belonged to, put together a list of things to tell children when they ask the hard questions like "Will we have to ride a boat again?" when the next afternoon shower happens. It is the kind of question asked in innocence we do not know what to say, some to slap the child until they never ask it again. They suggest this one answer: never promise what you cannot control and say "I will take care of you the best I can." It is an honest answer to an honest question. They do not deserve false promises or superman.

Interestingly, the superheroes of today were created during the great depression as was the game Monopoly with piles of play money. That is the kind of ingenuity my city needs. Hope in a dark time. I offer the song "Comeback" by Danny Gokey as my theme song for my own struggle, to the masses. In the comments of the video that has a practicing gymnast, there was the sentence, "She falls too much," said in innocence of not ever facing something as big as this. She did not fall too much. She did not fall enough or lose her legs the way others do to have to come back from. She did not lose her city either, she got up and tried it again. That is what we need to do. Allow Jesus to multiply the loaves and fishes hiding in secret baskets from the lowly and the fearful and the broken too. Every. One. The solutions the naysayers say won't work and the others who want things to stay the same. It will not be the same, ever. It will be a new normal that will one day bring great pride.

Then a text comes for a mandatory evacuation of a town nearby when my son lives. It strikes fear in me with the line "we may not be able to rescue anyone". My insides are trembling. Where are my adult children? Right away, I grab Gods word to me earlier, 'keep your eyes on me.' The tremble that began, stopped.

More comforting words come to me, 'what you can do is enough'. I like that. Everyone's small bit is enough. It always has been. Though some aspire to great things, greatness is not what this is about. Not for me, not for anyone in my city today. It is known for its compassion. I think it will eventually makes us the third largest city in America depending on how we handle ourselves between each other in the next days and weeks.

Just the same my heart is breaking as this cleansing is happening to me. Is this what is happening for the city? My mind cannot think that big. One at a time is enough for me. It will be individual decisions that matter, not just the governmental decisions and the officials.

I went out on the porch. There was a man standing in the pouring rain looking at the creek, allowing himself to get completely drenched. There must be an element of disbelief to do that for so long. The TV weathermen are looking at the swath of dry air moving like a thumb and fingers around the storm as if to squeeze it dry. Now it is really like the hand of God now. They hope aloud that the end of the rain will be tonight. It looks promising. The new map shows the rain gone tomorrow.

I decided to go back out on the porch and listen to the music of the rainfall. It feels good. Though I would like to wash my clothes and have a hot dinner, yeah that's pretty much it. It is good to hear the rhythm of the rain.

As I sat listening to the rain, I asked God where I will start my new work. He was plain and simple,

 'Here' he said.

He sent me here for a reason. I knew that 9 months ago and I saw the sign that said "Free Rent," in real need myself. Feeling better, I tried to start my work earlier. They could not give me a place to meet, though liked the idea. I will start where I can, with what I can... in God's direction and timing.

I am so overwhelmed with the news reports, I shut it off for a time to replenish myself. The ducks have sought refuge near the buildings in the puddles around the apartment complex instead of the quiet creek that is flooded. Small branches are falling in today's gust of wind, one large one is mistletoe, amazingly enough. It grows on the trees here like the Spanish moss does, in large ball like clusters. I always seek refuge in Christmas during a time like this. Sometimes it is enough to just think about it. This time I have been writing about it. Now it has come to me in a simple branch of mistletoe. I went outside and retrieved one for my living room. I want to put a tag on it, 'Merry Christmas Love, Harvey', hurricane Harvey, that is. Though it really is a sign from God that all is well and he is watching over me.

<u>Reality Again</u>

This storm is not giving up. It is back over water and headed east. The swath of dry air is pushing the storm east. It is going to make landfall again. It is projected to be going to the east and on to Louisiana. It could be the last day. The eye will not be going over us after all.

I went on Facebook and so many were praying for me and looking for me? Geeze, four days in and I am almost a missing person. Getting flooded in does that. I followed the directions, stay home and off the streets, who knew?

I went to take out the trash, there is toilet paper on the walk...is it a backup already of the system? The trash dumpster is getting full. The water went down in my street. They lost a police officer to the flood. He was on his way to work and drove into the water by accident. It has taken the wind out of the mayor and others.

Everyone copes in different ways with the crisis all around. There is a party atmosphere that ignites around here from time to time. Though the enthusiasm is waning. It feels like a bad dream. There are more private boats rescuing people than the national guard and all. It is amazing how many people have boats and waders. The officials are not complaining at all, everyone is pitching in together.

I notice too that cabin fever is taking hold of people, so is blame and anger for design of water drainage. Water drainage for 50+

inches was never anticipated. It is very emotional. It is hard to stay cooped up together with so many days inside. There are looting reports. Desperate people do desperate things. The changes all around will make people make new lives. Some will go willingly. Some will go kicking and screaming into their new normal. The sense of loss is all around.

<u>The Storm is Over</u>

I am one of the lucky ones. It is morning after the fifth night. I went to bed really early and slept about nine hours, straight through. It is windy today but going out will be possible. I have plans to go to out and look around. I am so sad for my city it is beyond words, though I have been trying for paragraphs. I walk around the neighborhood, then home. McDonalds is open, not much else.

At home I looked for some place to rest myself. I turn on the Christian channel, it is gone, for now. I look through and find one, Daystar playing praise music softly with scriptures in it. There it is...a place to rest. I cry. I want to call them. I finally did but cried anyway. She prayed with me. It helped me with my inner environment to calm myself with the calm music and talk to someone that gets it.

I took a walk as i was inspired to from Steven Furtick, on a channel that finally came back on. He talked about shooting a bow and how God is the power that makes it happen. He talked about how God plans the trajectory. It makes me think of my new life I am preparing for. One thing he did not say but I saw what this. God has to pull the bow string backward to give it the power it needs. So here I am pulled backwards again, sigh. It is by design.

I went to pay bills and get food. I was able to do it all. I am amazed. What was weird was I could see the potential in what was left on the store shelves that others couldn't. The ones that were having the hardest time were the privileged. They expected the store to have what they wanted and for it to be where it always is. It did not matter that the storm had ravaged everything. They could not go easy on the people working. They could not see potential in what was left.

For me, it is how I live these days, seeing the potential in the simple and what is left. I saw the garbage trucks making their rounds. I was delighted. There were so many businesses cleaning up and getting ready to open. I was sure to thank a few people in the store...the ladies making tortillas, the lady getting everyone in line, the man mopping the store floor. It is tremendously hard work today with many more demands than usual for them. They looked weary at 11:30am.

This story is not finished. It has taken amazing turns. God is still in control. What could the next chapter be?

Furniture Delivery and Finishing my Place

I called about the furniture delivery and find that Houston is closed to all commercial trucks for two weeks. My order is not even in town, in the warehouse. That is good really. It means it wasn't ruined and had to be manufactured again. I have to sit back and wait on it. It will be worth it when it comes. I look forward to having a couch and chairs and a bedframe with a headboard. I didn't really expect to get it five days from now as ordered. Now I know a little how it works when there is a hurricane. I know now all the trucks I see are supplies to meet the basic needs of Houston, all kinds of disaster relief. It is touching.

I think about how God wanted me to finish my place. There are some small things to get, still. Like a few teal pieces to decorate with, towels, kitchen gadgets to cook with, some fabric and polyester fiberfill. It could be complete before the furniture comes. It is very simple living.

Letting go of the old is supposed to hurt. It makes us appreciate the rebuilding even more for when it is finished, whether it is a house or things you like to do that are changing. I am with you on this... but just a little ahead.

Surprised

My son came over. He saw the first group of furniture in place
and things on the wall. I sent him to look at the bedroom. He
was impressed. He could not believe how it was even possible. I
told him I thought so too. This is really nice furniture he said. He
laid on the floor and watched the TV. I did not have another
chair yet. He seemed okay there. I did some hand sewing. He
chatted about the storm. He would remark about the furniture
and how was it even possible from time to time. I did not
explain anything. I let him take it in. He was too astonished to
take anything else in.

Going Home

I can't believe it. I was resting and trying to settle in for the night and I felt the message in me, 'you are going home'. I knew I was here temporarily. I did not know how long it would be. I fought with all I had to not settle in. I knew I would not be staying. Yet this project required me to. I have a lot of questions now like...what will my "after" look like? Will my new stuff look right in my new place? What about the curtains, will they fit the windows? I was assured that God had it covered. Of course he does. God is so confusing like that about his plans for me. Just when I think I know what is going on, he changes it. I believe him. I just do. I am so glad I do not have to bring all that old stuff with me and get to bring the new. Yes, I do know where home is. It is not temporary like this one. Yet I know I am to make the best of it while still here and not try to wish it away. There may still be a few blessings left I do not want to miss.

After...

It took quite a bit of trust to take on this project, a trust in God I have never had. I just never thought of it in times of plenty. This season of my life has caused me to become fully dependent on him. It could have resulted in nothing and I was okay with that, hence the folding furniture of my disbelief. But I gave it all to him, every bit of it...not knowing what would happen. What did he do? Give me something beautiful that I did not expect. Just the kind of thing that others can understand as I begin to tell my story and do my new work he gave me. I feel so loved it is difficult to express. It feels so good to be in the palm of God's hand.

Where are the Photos?

I wanted to have before and after photos for this book. There is a problem with that. It will make the book a lot more expensive. I need to get the word out to those who do not really have the means for a book with color photos. Another reason is that my results could disappoint. Many people have ideas about what a great environment looks like. That does not matter at all in this. What matters is you get to build for you...high end, middle range, or what you found on the corner to refurbish. IT DOES NOT MATTER. Not one bit, what mine looks like. What matters is that you have something just right for you. If you reach for God, he will not disappoint, not ever.

"He will raise you up on eagle's wings, bear you on the breath of dawn. Make you to shine like the sun...and hold you in the palm of his hand."

Not Finished

This project is not finished, sad but true. The storm has delayed things, of course. Already there are sales going on for furniture. I expect to finish this project but not in the time frame I thought I would. It is about availability at this point. Yet I know that God will show me the way. I will finish it, somehow. It is going to be wonderful. It really is. It is more important that you know my secret to how to do this...besides, I am going home and what that will entail, I do not know. That's how God works, there is always a little bit more.

Part 3: Put it to the Test

Nuts as it sounds, it could sound like an ordinary makeover. Yet the thought has come to me to invite you to test it for yourself. God himself has asked people to do that over the millennia. If you are a skeptic, then go for it. He has such big things for you, it would amaze you. Why not start with this?

Too often we put trust in ourselves and our own successes. We do and have done everything humanly possible. Some of us have reached great heights using that method. Some of us are at our lowest lows. Some of us are complacent and happy about it. Some are in a rut and hate it. Just think how nice it would be to have a whole new space to nurture the new you. It's fabulous. I am still marveling.

It is an exercise in trust him fully. It is an exercise in how many small details really matter to him. It is an exercise of following his timing on something. It is an exercise of doing something you don't know what the end result will be. It is an exercise of following him down rabbit holes to something that looks like a waste of time. It is an exercise in buying things you do not know what they are for until later. It is an exercise in the adventure of what it really means to follow God by actually doing something besides listening in church and putting your offering in the plate. It is a warm up to a life of action, to do your calling, to be truly a light for others. Ask those around you who have a relationship with God, does he ask them to do the unusual? He does. Did Jesus do the unusual? Yes, he did. Does God really give directions? He does. As early in the bible as Genesis and the Garden of Eden, then on to Moses moving the Israelites, then to the passion of Jesus, then to the disciples running about the countryside spreading the gospel. Do you think they thought of all that on their own? Absolutely not. They all had directions, every single one of them and many more after them. You could be one of them too, in modern times as a new "doubting Thomas", who wants to see it for himself or herself. This is your chance, go for it.

As for those who want to contact me and argue with me it isn't so, I will not be answering your messages no matter how many you send or how it reaches me. By the way, how did you find the way to read all the way to the end of this book? Yeah, there is something in it tickling your fancy, there is. It will be waiting. God will be waiting.

As for me, I won't be. I have better things to do for God. I am off on my next adventure. I wonder how God will top this one? See, it is working for me already. Who is this woman with fire in her who used to be so quiet and reserved about so many things?

Just me, and am surprising myself every day.

I did it. You could too.

As for the storm, I wrote a lot of this book before hurricane Harvey. I decided to keep the book as it was. It provides a place to begin after a disaster, large scale or personal. It shows the way in a time of uncertainty and how good God is. I had no idea how poignant and timely the topic would be later in the project. God did. It feels like a chance of a lifetime now. Who could argue that?

Blessed be.

Susan

Appendices: Shopping Lists

My hope in providing this list is that it might give you some direction on simple living, something you just might do for a time after experience your own disaster, and give you some direction about what you might need. It is a place to begin when the overwhelm hits. Do not forget to pray and ask God for his directions and assistance at every juncture. His ideas are the best.

Appendix A: Furniture Shopping list

Furniture: Group 1

mattress and box spring

black chair

sofa table

large shelf

Furniture: Group 2

Couch

2 chairs

bedframe and headboard

Gently Used:

2 barstools

<u>Refurbished:</u>

Square Trunk, painted teal

Appendix B: Den Shopping List

<u>Purchased:</u>

9 clocks and a poster

<u>Reused:</u>

3 drawer organizer

picture fames and degrees

poster frame

Appendix C: Bedroom Shopping List

<u>Purchased:</u>

Comforter and Pillow Sham Set

Sheet Set

2 standard pillows

1 decorative pillow

<u>Sewn:</u>

Curtain valance

<u>Refurbished:</u>

2 picture frames, painted teal

Appendix D: Living Room Shopping List

<u>purchased new</u>:

decorative globe

picture frames for family photos

small milk bottles, 4

<u>gently used</u>:

book stand, metal

antique ice skates

<u>Reused</u>:

Small TV

DVD Player

Videos and music

memorabilia from places I have been

mirror tiles, left over from another project

Appendix E: Kitchen Shopping List

Purchased New:

Convection Toaster Oven

Covered Dutch Oven

Large skillet

Small skillet

covered 2 quart pot

Square plates, 2 place settings

Tasting plates: 2 sizes, 4 inch and 2 inch

Drinkware: tumblers, tea glasses, juice glasses

Knives: 1 large, I medium, 1 bread knife

Cooking Tools: 2 rubber pancake turners, 2 wood spatulas, 1 spatula. wisk. pastry brush

Baking: 2, 3 inch ramekins

measuring cup set

2 placemats

Sewn:

Curtains

Reused:

hand held spiralizer

Appendix F: Bathroom Shopping List

<u>Sewn</u>:

Shower Curtain

Window Curtain

Appendix G: Wish List

These are the remainder of the items needed to complete my place:

coffee table

lamps to read by

vacuum cleaner

silverware and caddy

vegetable peeler

the remainder of the dishes: salad plates, bowls, mugs

measuring spoons

caddy for stirring implements

tongs

bottle opener

ladle

crock pot

grater

can opener

kitchen shears

fabric for the shower curtain and throw pillows, polyester fiberfill

towels and carpets

bin for toiletries

shower hooks

teal accent items for the shelf, one of them being a popcorn bowl

decorative trunk

black storage ottoman

2 11x17 black frames to frame the maps

jars for spices

canisters

angled measuring cups

oil dispensers

paper towel holder

trash can

outdoor furniture for the porch and potted plant

inside the closet work spaces: 2 work tables, 2 lamps, 2 extension cords

3 plastic boxes to protect the memorabilia

30" X 28" frame for another map

2" binder

Appendix H: Hurricane Food Shopping

precooked frozen burger patties

walnut halves and pieces

mesquite sliced ham

mixed frozen vegetables

cups of diced peaches

wheat tortillas (freshly made in the store)

hummus

small apples

vanilla yogurt cups

vegetable crackers

What did I make out of this?

yogurt with peaches and walnuts

wraps

soup

tacos

cracker snacks

To find out more about this topic see my yellow cover food and recipe books and the other yellow over books help with living simply too. It is more than good enough for every day.

Back Cover:

This author has come to realize that environments are about more than beauty and more than functionality. It is more than a place to eat, sleep, and rest. It is more than safety from the elements. Where one lives matters. It is even hardest in times of transition to something new and not knowing what to expect or which direction to go.

Faced with a decision like that, she turned to God who filled her in on how to begin her new life by giving the task of decorating her apartment. It was a new twist on the problem she did not expect. She could decorate for who she was to become, if she trusted him fully. She decided to do it knowing only God had that information.

Included are the secrets and the struggle to do so. It involved hunting, and stepping out of one's comfort zone. It involved waiting on the timing for when and where to go seek what she needed, an unusual approach indeed and one she would gladly do again.

"It feels so good to be in the palm of God's hand in even the smallest of things. I thought God was like a big human man, scratching his head trying to understand me. Nope, I am made in his image and he fully gets it. It matters to him what my environment looks like. It matters a lot because it matters to me. He put that desire in me there."

Part way through the project, in blew hurricane Harvey. What happened to the project? You have got to find out how good

God is as he started on the author's inside environment...as her city recovers and home items become available once again.

Here is the process of how it went for her. Take the chance. It might be more fun and enlightening than you think.